P9-CKE-853

Brazilian
phrasebook

Mark Balla

Brazilian Phrasebook
  1st edition

Published by
  Lonely Planet Publications
  Head Office: PO Box 617, Hawthorn, Victoria 3122, Australia
  US Office: PO Box 2001A, Berkeley, CA 94702, USA

Printed by
  Colorcraft Ltd, Hong Kong

Published
  March 1990

Editor	Chris Taylor
Design	Peter Flavelle
Cover illustration	Ann Jeffree
Illustrations	Ralph Roob
Typesetting	Tricia Giles

National Library of Australia Cataloguing in Publication Data

Balla, Mark
  Brazilian phrasebook

  ISBN 0 86442 068 4.

  1. Portuguese language – Brazil – Conversation and phrase books
  – English. I. Title.

469. 798
© Copyright Lonely Planet 1990

All rights reserved. No part of this publication may be reproduced, stored in a
retrieval system or transmitted in any form by any means, electronic,
mechanical, photocopying, recording or otherwise, except brief extracts for the
purpose of review, without the written permission of the publisher and
copyright owner.

Contents

Introduction

Brazil has a population of some 130 million, almost all of whom speak Portuguese (or *brasileiro* as it is known by many). Those who don't speak the national language are either recent immigrants or members of certain isolated Indian tribes in the Amazon region. Around the borders of Uruguay and Argentina there are Spanish-speaking communities and, near the Paraguayan border, there are speakers of Guaraní, one of Paraguay's two national languages.

There have been a number of developments in the Portuguese language since the Portuguese arrived around the beginning of the 16th century. The main changes are related to vocabulary and pronunciation and came about due to various African and Indian influences – influences that were also important in the development of Brazilian culture. African influences, brought about by the slave trade with Portugal's colonies of São Tomé, Guinea-Bissau, Angola and other coastal regions of Africa, can be felt today in, among other things, the music of Brazil. Other influences are present in the large Japanese and Korean communities of São Paulo and Rio states and, further south, in European communities from countries such as Germany and Italy.

Brazilians are famous for their parties and no discussion of Brazil would be complete without a mention of *carnaval*. This is not limited to Rio de Janeiro. In fact, you would be hard pressed to find a city or town which does not get caught up in this madcap week of lunacy. Processions, dancing, all-night partying, drinking and general debauchery almost

5

bring the country to a stand-still for nearly a week of festivities unrivalled by any on the planet. In reality the partying begins long before and ends weeks after the official carnaval period.

Finally, it has become very fashionable of late for wealthier Brazilians to take courses in English at one of the numerous private language schools that have sprung up throughout the country. However, with so little opportunity to practice, there are not many people outside the major cities who can get by in English. Certainly the foreigner who has any Portuguese is a step ahead of the rest.

Pronunciation

Portuguese pronunciation can be rather tricky for English speakers. Certainly the only way to acquire perfect pronunciation is to spend a considerable amount of time in a Portuguese-speaking country. Nevertheless, if this guide is carefully followed, you should have no problems being understood.

Vowels

Without a doubt the most frustrating thing in learning to pronounce Portuguese is the vowels. As will be seen in the 'Diphthongs' section, the following list consists of only general rules.

a as the 'u' in 'up'
e at the beginning or at the end of a word, as the 'ee' in 'feet', only shorter; elsewhere as the 'e' in 'pet'
i as the 'ee' in 'feet', only shorter
o at the end of a word or before an **e**, as the 'u' in 'put', only shorter; elsewhere as the 'o' in 'or'
u as the 'u' in 'put'

Nasalisation

When a tilde appears over a vowel (eg **ã**), this means that the vowel should be heavily nasalised. This is done by allowing air to escape through the nose when you are pronouncing the

7

vowel. The sound produced is very similar to the sound you get when you hold your nose and talk. Basically the best way to learn is to listen to Brazilians speaking, and then just practise until you get it right.

Diphthongs

Most diphthongs, or combinations of vowels, are pronounced by following the general rules for vowels, and simply pronouncing them one after the other in the order that they appear. All the same, there are a few that are worth noting.

ei as the 'ay' in 'day', but perhaps a little longer
oi as the 'oy' in 'boy'
ão as the 'ow' in 'how' (only nasalised)
õe nasalised version of **oi**

Stress

When a word ends in **r** or a nasalised vowel, the stress falls on the last syllable, unless there is an accent on one of the other vowels in the word.

If a vowel has either a circumflex accent (**ê**) or an acute (**é**) accent, the stress falls on that vowel no matter where it is in the word. In all other words the stress falls on the penultimate vowel (assuming the word has more than one syllable of course).

In the following list the stressed syllable is highlighted:

favor   favour
amanhã   tomorrow

órfã	orphan
você	you
lágrima	tear (from the eyes)
parágrafo	paragraph
porèm	however

Consonants

Most consonants in Portuguese are similar to their English counterparts, but there are exceptions. The good news is that the consonants are not as difficult to master as the vowels. Only those consonants which vary considerably from English will be discussed here. You can assume that you already know how to pronounce the others.

c	as the 'c' in 'cease' when it occurs before **e** or **i**; elsewhere, as the 'k' in 'kiss'
ç	as the 'c' in 'cease'
d	as the 'j' in 'jungle' when followed by **e** or **i**; elsewhere as the 'd' in 'dog'
g	as the 'g' in 'rouge' when it occurs before **e** or **i**; elsewhere as the 'g' in 'game'
h	not pronounced (note **lh** and **nh** following)
j	as the 'g' in 'rouge'
l	after a vowel, something like the 'l' in 'pool', only a bit more like a 'w'; elsewhere, as a regular English 'l'
lh	as the 'lli' in 'million'
m & n	after a vowel, the vowel is nasalised, and the **m** or the **n** is not articulated – a little like the 'ng' in 'sing'; elsewhere, as in English
nh	as the 'ny' in 'canyon'
q	as the 'k' in 'keep'

qu	as 'qu' in 'quill' when followed by **a** or **o**; elsewhere like an English 'k'
r	at the beginning or end of a word as **rr** (see below); elsewhere as a short rolled 'r'
rr	as an English 'h', only with more friction; a little softer than a French 'r' (occasionally you may hear it rolled depending on which part of the country you are in)
s	as the 's' in 'star' before a vowel; before **p**, **t**, **k**, or at the end of a word, as the 'sh' in 'ship'; elsewhere as the 'z' in 'zoo', only a little softer
ss	as the 's' in 'star'
t	as the 'ch' in 'chair' when followed by **e** or **i**; elsewhere as the 't' in 'table'
x	as the 'sh' in 'ship' when it occurs at the beginning of a word or comes after **e** or **i**; elsewhere as the 'x' in 'taxi'

Grammar

Word Order

In general, Portuguese word order is similar to English word order. For example:

(Eu) *queiro* *telefonar* *aos* *Estados Unidos.*
I   want to telephone to the USA (States United).

Meu *nome* *é* *Marcos.*
My name is Mark.

As in English, word order is subject-verb-object. You will notice that the name for the USA is 'States United'. This is the most obvious difference in word order between Portuguese and English – the adjective comes after the noun. For example:

(Eu) *estou* *procurando* *um* *hôtel* *muito* *barato.*
I am looking for a hotel very cheap.

Furthermore, you will notice that the word for 'I' is in brackets in the examples given here. This is because it is not usually necessary to include pronouns in sentences where grammatical context makes their identity obvious. As you will find in the section on verbs, the form of the verb tells you who or what the speaker is talking about. Of course, if you want to include the pronoun that is fine.

11

We are going to Rio de Janeiro tomorrow.
 (Nós) vamos ao Rio de Janeiro amanhã.
I am hungry.
 (Eu) estou com fôme.

Questions

Questions are often identical to statements, with the exception that the intonation changes. This is done much the same as in English, with a kind of inquisitive rise in the voice at the end of the question.

Are we going to Rio de Janeiro tomorrow?
 (Nós) vamos ao Rio de Janeiro amanhã?

Question Words

where	Where is the Australian Embassy?
onde	*Onde fica a embaixada australiana?*
when	When is it necessary to renew my visa?
quando	*Quando é preciso renovar meu visto?*
why	Why are we stopping here?
por que	*Por que estamos parando aqui?*
what	What's wrong?/What's the matter?
(o) que	*O que é?/Que é?*
how, by what means	How do I find the bus station from here?
como é que	*Como é que encontro a rodoviaria daqui?*

who	Who are you?
quem	*Quem é voçê?*
which/what (one)	What is the best restaurant in the city?
qual	*Qual é o melhor restaurante da cidade?*
which/what (ones)	Which are the best bars in the city?
quais	*Quais são os melhores bares da cidade?*

Nouns

Plurals

In general nouns are made plural by adding an *s*. For example:

cat	*gato*
cats	*gatos*
pen	*caneta*
pens	*canetas*

If the noun ends in *s*, *z* or *r*, and that syllable is stressed, then the plural is formed by adding *es*. For example:

woman	*mulher*
women	*mulheres*
Englishman	*inglés*
Englishmen	*ingléses*
youth	*rapaz*
youths	*rapazes*

Gender

There are four definite articles in Portuguese. They are:

a	feminine singular (the)	*a mulher* – the woman
as	feminine plural (the)	*as mulheres* – the women
o	masculine singular (the)	*o homen* – the man
os	masculine plural (the)	*os homens* – the men

There are also four indefinite articles in Portuguese:

uma	feminine singular (a, one)	*uma menina* – a girl
umas	feminine plural (some)	*umas meninas* – some girls
um	masculine singular (a, one)	*um menino* – a boy
uns	masculine plural (some)	*uns meninos* – some boys

There are some guidelines by which you can determine the gender of some nouns, but most of these 'rules' have exceptions.

Nouns ending with *-dade* are feminine:

a universidade
  (the) university

Nouns ending with *-ão* are feminine:

a mão
  (the) hand

Nouns ending with -*a* are feminine:

a música
(the) music

Nouns ending with -*o* are masculine:

o facho
(the) torch

Adjectives

Adjectives take the same gender and number as the noun which they describe. They are generally placed after the noun:

a cold beer (beer cold)	*uma cerveja fria*
the beautiful beaches (beaches beautifuls)	*as praias bonitas*
the white wine (wine white)	*o vinho branco*
an American bank (bank American)	*um banco americano*

Pronouns
Personal Pronouns

I	*eu*
me	*mim*
you (singular)	*você*
he/him/it (masculine)	*ele*
she/her/it (feminine)	*ela*
we/us	*nós*
you (plural)	*vocês*

they/them (masculine) *eles*
they/them (feminine) *elas*

Possessive Pronouns

Possessive pronouns work like adjectives in that they take
the gender and number of the noun which they modify. The
following table gives both the masculine and feminine
singular forms of the relevant possessive pronouns. The
plural forms are made by adding *s*.

	masculine	feminine
my	*meu*	*minha*
your (singular)	*seu*	*sua*
his/her	*seu*	*sua*
our	*nosso*	*nossa*
your (plural)	*seu*	*sua*
their (m/f)	*seu*	*sua*

Remember that possessive pronouns do not vary according
to the gender of the possessor, but according to that of the
possessed.

Possession can also be expressed by using *de* (of) followed
by the relevant personal pronoun or a noun. *De* is contracted
to *d* where the personal pronoun begins with a vowel.

The backpack is his.
   A mochila é dele. or *É sua mochila.*
It is their (the girls) car.
   O carro é delas. or *É seu carro.*
It's my passport.
   O passaporte é de mim. or *É meu passaporte.*

Madalena's house is near here.
A casa de Madalena está perto.

It can sometimes be an advantage to use *de* plus a personal pronoun, as this makes the possessor easier to identify.

Verbs

Verbs, due to their complexity, are probably the aspect of Portuguese that English speakers have the greatest difficulty in mastering. Firstly, there are three standard kinds of regular verbs (*-ar*, *-er*, and *-ir*). In addition, there are the double stemmed *-iar* and *-ear* verbs and the so-called two-stem *-ir* verbs. Finally, there are the irregular verbs.

So before even contemplating the various tenses and verb forms, there are seven types of verb to cope with. Each of these verb types has 23 possible forms. In all that comes to a horrifying grand total of 161 possible forms.

Fortunately, only a few of these are essential. Basically all that a traveller needs to know is how to form the future, present and past tenses. The present participle (-ing form) is also useful, and fairly easy as well.

To Be

Portuguese has two verbs which translate as 'to be' in English: *ser* and *estar*. For an English speaker to master these two completely can take years, but to grasp the basic differences is not too difficult.

Ser

The verb *ser* is an irregular verb, which means that there are no simple rules to follow in declining it. The present tense is declined as follows:

I am	*eu sou*
you are, he/she is	*você, ele/ela é*
we are	*nós somos*
they are	*eles/elas são*

This verb refers to states which have a degree of permanency or durability about them. For example:

My name is Mark.
  Meu nome é Marcos.
I am Australian.
  Sou Australiano.

There is an implication that the states referred to in these two examples will not change.

Estar

The verb *estar*, also meaning 'to be', generally refers to events which are temporary in nature. It is also irregular, but not terribly difficult to learn:

I am	*eu sou*
you are, he/she is	*você, ele/ela é*
we are	*nós estamos*
they are	*eles/elas estão*

Here are some examples of how *estar* is used:

I am lost.
  Estou perdido.
My friend is ill.
  Meu amigo está doente.

There is an implication that the states referred to in these two examples may change.

Tenses
Preliminaries
As stated in the introduction to the Verbs section, there are seven kinds of verbs. Of these, only three kinds will be discussed here: -*ar*, -*er* and -*ir* verbs. The other kinds will have to be learned on an individual basis (particularly the irregular verbs). However, if the rules given here are followed for all verbs, you will be understood in almost all cases.

Present
The most important thing in forming the present tense of a verb is to find the stem of the verb by removing its ending (-*ar*, -*er*, -*ir*, etc). For example:

	infinitive	stem
to dwell (in a place)	*morar*	*mor*-
to eat	*comer*	*com*-
to leave	*partir*	*part*-

To form the present tense, various endings are added to the stem, but the endings vary depending on whether the verb ends in -*ar*, -*er* or -*ir*:

infinitive	*morar*	*comer*	*partir*
stem	*mor*-	*com*-	*part*-
I	-*o*	-*o*	-*o*
he/she/it/you (singular)	-*a*	-*e*	-*e*
we	-*amos*	-*emos*	-*imos*
they/you (plural)	-*am*	-*em*	-*em*

Some examples:

They live in Australia.
Eles moram na Austrália.
We are leaving now.
Nós partimos agora.
I do not eat meat.
Eu não como carne.

Future

The simplest way to form the future tense is to add the following endings to the infinitive:

I	*-ei*
he/she/you (singular)	*-á*
we	*-emos*
they	*-ão*

These future tense verb endings are stressed. In the following examples, the stressed syllable has been highlighted:

I will leave tomorrow.
*Eu partir**ei** amanhã.*
You will eat beans every day in Brazil.
*Você comer**á** feijão todos os dias no Brasil.*
We will sleep well tonight.
*Nos dormir**emos** bem hoje a noite.*
They will go to São Paulo in the morning.
*Eles/elas ir**ão** para São Paulo na manhã.*

The future tense can also be formed by using the present tense of the verb *ir* (to go) followed by the infinitive of the relevant verb. An irregular verb, *ir* is particularly useful and not very difficult:

I am going to leave tomorrow.
 Eu vou partir amanhã.
You are going to eat beans every day in Brazil.
 Voçê vai comer feijão todos os dias no Brasil.
We are going to sleep well tonight.
 Nós vamos dormir bem hoje a noite.
They are going to go to São Paulo in the morning.
 Eles vão ir para São Paulo na manhã.

Past

This is the most difficult concept to pick up in Portuguese. There are three fairly important ways of referring to the past, and it is necessary to have some idea about at least two of them. In both cases the tense is formed by adding endings to the stem of the verb.

If you want to talk about something that is over and done with, then you should add the following endings to the stems:

verb type	-ar	-er	-ir
I	-ei	-í	-í
he/she/it/you (singular)	-ou	-eu	-iu
we	-amos	-emos	-imos
they/you (plural)	-ram	-ram	-ram

Some examples:

I lived in the USA for one year.
 Eu morei nos Estados Unidos durante um ano.

They ate five times yesterday.
Eles comeram cinco vezes ontem.
That man followed Helena yesterday.
Este homem segiu a Helena ontem.

If you want talk about something in the past which may not necessarily have finished (have a look at the examples after the table and you'll find this idea easier to follow), then you should add the following endings to the verb stems:

verb type	-ar	-er	-ir
I	*-ava*	*-ia*	*-ia*
he/she/it/you (singular)	*-ava*	*-ia*	*-ia*
we	*-avamos*	*-íamos*	*-íamos*
they/you (plural)	*-avam*	*-iam*	*-iam*

Some examples:

I have lived in Australia for the last three years. (and am still here)
Eu morava na Austrália para os últimos trés anos.
They have eaten five times today. (and may eat again)
Eles comiam cinco vezes hoje.
That man has followed Helena many times. (and may do so again)
Este homem seguia a helena muitas vezes.

Greetings & Civilities

Greetings

Hello.
  Olá.
Good morning.
  Bom dia. (relatively formal)
Good afternoon/evening.
  Boa tarde. (after midday)
Good evening/night.
  Boa noite. (after dark)
Hi.
  Oi. (informal, friendly)

All of these greetings (especially the last) are often followed
by the question *todo bem?* (or *todo bom?*), which is
something like 'how's things?' or 'how's it going?'. This
question doesn't have to be answered, but it would be
impolite not to respond to the greeting.

Hi. How's it going?
  Oi. todo bom?
How are you?
  Como esta?
  Como vai?
I'm well, thanks.
  Vou bem, obrigado/a.

23

When someone enquires about your health, as in most countries, there is an expectation that you will respond positively and leave it at that.

Some Useful Words

good	*bom*
bad	*mau*
terrible	*ruim* (a favourite among Brazilians) or *terrivel*

Goodbyes

Goodbye.
　Ciao. (informal)
　Adeus. (formal, more final than *ciao*)
See you soon.
　Até logo.
See you later.
　Até já.
Until we meet again. (informal)
　Até a proxima.

Forms of Address

Senhor functions as 'Mr', 'Sir' and even 'Lord', as in 'The Lord's Prayer'.

O senhor is something like 'gentleman'. It is commonly used when enquiring about someone's health in a particularly respectful manner:

How are you sir? (How is the gentleman?)
　Como vai o senhor?

Senhora functions as Mrs, Madam(e) or Ma'am.
A senhora is something like 'lady'. It is also common when
  asking respectfully about someone's health:

How are you Ma'am? (How is the lady?)
  Como vai a senhora?

Rapaz is like 'young man'.
Senhorinha and, to a lesser extent, *senhorita* are used in
  Brazil as equivalents of 'Miss', but they are not
  particularly widespread.
Menina is a young lady or a little girl.
Moça is also used like *menina*, although it tends to be a little
  less respectful as it often refers to a live-in maid.
Rapariga in Portugal means 'girl'. It should not be used in
  Brazil, however, as it is extremely disrespectful.

Other Civilities
please
  por favor

Males and females have different ways of saying
'thankyou'.

thankyou (females)
  obrigada
thankyou (males)
  obrigado
many thanks (females)
  muita obrigada
many thanks (males)
  muito obrigado

no problem/that's alright/think nothing of it, etc
   de nada
sorry
   disculpa
Can you forgive me?
   Me disculpa?
excuse me (eg when leaving the table)
   com licença

'Uncivilities'

These are very much a part of life in Brazil, but as a foreigner you have to be careful not to use them inappropriately. If you are with Brazilian friends in an informal environment, you will probably have them rolling on the floor in delight. If you are talking with the receptionist at the Meridien Hotel in Rio, things could become a little unpleasant. Take care.

Estou fodido – If you have had a really hard day, and want someone to know that you are absolutely exhausted, try this one.

Está fodido – If something is not working, whether it is your plans, your camera, your mind, or whatever, this one is pretty useful.

Merda! – Shit!

Porra! – Similar to 'Wow!'. It can also be used to indicate irritation.

Virgem maria! or *Vixe maria!* – These two refer to the Virgin Mary. They are usually uttered as an expression of surprise or even wonder. Disgust is another emotion that can be expressed by these two. Tone of voice is of the essence. They are more common in the northern regions of the country.

Small Talk

In conversation Brazilians utilise almost every part of their bodies, perhaps to an even greater extent than do Italians. Many westerners (particularly of the English speaking variety) feel uncomfortable when speaking with Brazilians, complaining that they stand too close when talking. Brazilian women often have trouble with western men who almost invariably misread their body-language.

Outside the larger cities, where there are not as many travellers, people will be genuinely interested in you and your country.

What is your name?
   Como é seu nome?
My name is ....
   Meu nome é ....

Nationalities

If someone asks you where you are from, the answer depends on the gender and number of your country. For example, Brazil is masculine singular (*o Brasil*), whereas the USA is masculine plural (*os Estados Unidos*). Australia is feminine singular (*a Austrália*), and the Philippines are feminine plural (*as Filipinas*). As it happens, most countries are feminine singular, but there are too many exceptions for this to be a rule.

So if you are from the USA, you would say *sou dos Estados Unidos*; a Canadian would say *sou da Canada*; and someone from the UK would say *sou do Reino Unido*.

Where are you from?	*De onde vem?*
I am from	*Sou d*.......
Argentina	*a Argentina*
Australia	*a Austrália*
Brazil	*o Brasil*
Canada	*a Canada*
Chile	*o Chile*
Denmark	*a Dinamarca*
England	*a Inglaterra*
Finland	*a Finlândia*
France	*a França*
Germany	*a Alemania*
Ireland	*a Irlânda*
Israel	*a Israel*
Italy	*a Italia*
Japan	*o Japão*
New Zealand	*a Nova zelânda*
Norway	*a Noruega*
Paraguay	*a Paraguai*
Peru	*o Perú*
Scotland	*a Escocia*
Sweden	*a Suecia*
Switzerland	*a Suiça*

the Philippines	*as Filipinas*
the UK	*o Reino Unido*
the USA	*os Estados Unidos*

Professions

What is your profession?
Qué é a sua profissão?
What do you do?
Qué é que você faz?
Where do you work?
Onde é que você trabalha?

Where the name of an occupation ends in a consonant, the feminine form is created by the addition of an 'a'; where it ends in an 'o', turn the 'o' into an 'a'; other vowels remain the same for feminine forms.

My profession is	*Minha profissão é ....*
I am a/an	*Sou ....*
artist	*artista*
businessperson	*negociante*
doctor	*médico*
journalist	*jornalista*
lawyer	*advogado* (m)
	advogada (f)
mechanic	*mecánico* (m)
	mecánica (f)
nurse	*enfermeiro* (m)
	enfermeira (f)
plumber	*canalizador* (m)
	canalizadora (f)
student	*estudante*

teacher	*professor* (m)
	professora (f)
worker	*trabalhador* (m)
	trabalhadora (f)

Religion

The majority of Brazilians are catholics, but freedom of religion is guaranteed. Brazilian catholicism is heavily influenced by some forms of African animism due to the large number of people of African descent living in the country.

What is your religion?	*Qual é a sua religião?*
I am (a)	*Sou ....*
Anglican	*anglicano*
Buddhist	*budista*
Catholic	*católico*
Christian	*cristão*
Hindu	*hindú*
Jewish	*judeu*
Muslim	*muçulmano*
Protestant	*protestante*

Family

aunt	*tia*
brother	*irmão*
child	*criança*
cousin	*primo/a*
father	*pai*
father-in-law	*sogro*
husband	*esposo*

mother	*mãe*
mother-in-law	*sogra*
nephew	*sobrinho*
niece	*sobrinha*
sister	*irmã*
uncle	*tio*
wife	*esposa*

Languages

I do not speak Brazilian.
   Não falo brasileiro.
I do not understand.
   Não comprendo.
Could you repeat that please?
   Pode repetir por favor?
Could you please speak a little more slowly?
   Pode falar mais devagar por favor?

Do you speak ....?	*Você fala ....?*
I speak	*Eu falo ....*
Arabic	*árabe*
Brazilian/Portuguese	*brasileiro/português*
Danish	*dinamarqués*
English	*inglés*
French	*francés*
German	*alemão*
Italian	*italiano*
Japanese	*japonés*
Norwegian	*noruego*
Spanish	*espanhol*
Swedish	*sueco*

Some Useful Phrases

How old are you?
  Quantos anos você tem?
I am (25) years old. (see Numbers chapter)
  Tenho (vinte e cinco) anos.
Are you married?
  Você está casado/a?
Do you have any children?
  Você tem crianças?
Where do you live?
  Onde é que você mora?

Accommodation

The cost and standard of accommodation in Brazil can be incredibly varied. There are five-star hotels in Rio, São Paolo and Brasilia which are as expensive and luxurious as any in the world; while there are *barracas* (huts) in some of the smaller Amazonian towns which are nothing more than four posts holding up a thatched roof under which to sling your hammock.

Luxuries such as hot running water and flushing toilets cannot be guaranteed in any of the cheaper *hoteis* (hotels) and *pensões* (boarding houses), although most places south of Bahia tend to be more aware of the 'needs' of spoiled tourists. In the interior, the north-east and the north of Brazil, even the wealthier locals don't often have hot running water in their homes. But then, with the sometimes stifling humidity, a cold shower two or three times a day can be a real godsend.

The word *hotel* is also the generic term for any form of travellers' accommodation. Youth hostels are not very common in Brazil; they are generally found only in the larger cities of the south.

Finding Accommodation

I am looking for ....   *Estou procurando ....*
    a hotel   *um hotel*
    a youth hostel   *um albergue de*
                                    juventude

33

a boarding house   *uma pensão*
somewhere to spend the night   *onde passar a noite*

What is the best hotel in the city?
  Qual é a melhor hotel da cidade?
It must not be too expensive.
  Não deve ser muito caro.
I'm looking for a cheap hotel.
  Estou procurando um hotel barato.

At the Hotel

I would like a room please.
  Quero um quarto por favor.
Could I see the room?
  Posso ver o quarto?
How much does it cost per night/week?
  Quanto custa a noite/semana?
Don't you have anything cheaper?
  Não tem nada mas barato?
Is that with breakfast?
  É com a café da manhã?
Do you have full board?
  Tem pensão completa?
Does it have air-con?
  Está aire-acondicionado?

Complaints

The room is too noisy.
  O quarto é barulhoso demais.
The light doesn't work.
  A luz não funciona.

The room is dirty.
O quarto é sujo.
The fan is broken.
O ventilador está quebrado.

Some Useful Words

broken	*quebrado*
dark	*oscuro*
dirt	*sujeira*
dirty	*sujo*
noise	*barulho*
noisy	*barulhoso*
smell	*cheiro*

Some Useful Phrases

Does the room have a bathroom?
O quarto tem banheiro?
Is there hot water?
Tem agua quente?
Is the hot water turned on all day?
A agua quente esta ligado o dia enteiro?

I'd like a room with a good view.
Quero um quarto com uma boa vista.
I've lost the key to my room.
He perdido a chave do meu quarto.
Do you have a safe where I can leave my valuables?
Tem um cofre onde posso guardar minhas coisas de valor?
Could you make up my bill please?
Pode preparar minha conta por favor?
Do you accept credit cards?
Você aceita as cartas de crédito?

Some Useful Words

air-conditioning	*aire-acondicionado*
balcony	*balcão*
bath	*banho*
bathroom	*banheiro*
bed	*cama*
candle	*vela*
chair	*cadeira*
double bed	*cama matrimonial*
fan	*ventilador*
mirror	*espelho*
shower	*ducha*
soap	*sabonete*
table	*mesa*
toilet	*retrete* (the standard euphemism is *banheiro*)
toilet paper	*papel higénico*
towel	*toalha*
wardrobe	*guarda-roupa*
window	*janela*

Warning: beware of hotels (especially north of Bahia) which have hot showers. The heating systems are usually very primitive. More often than not the system is inside the shower rose, which is simply plugged into a socket in the wall. No-one in Brazil has ever thought of earthing electrical appliances, so it can be positively dangerous to have a hot shower. The best thing to do is to unplug the shower rose before you have a shower. If you can't face a cold shower, it might not be a bad idea to wear a pair of rubber thongs (flip-flops) for hot showers.

Getting Around

In general, the car driver is king of the road. Other vehicles and pedestrians are shown no mercy, and certainly no courtesy. Driving is not policed, and traffic violations are unheard of. Nevertheless, despite all appearances to the contrary, Brazil, in theory at least, does hold to the convention that a red light is a signal to stop.

Watch out at night for cars driving without headlights. It's also always a good idea to slow down as you enter a town; many have *quebra-molas* (speed bumps) which you don't see until it's too late.

Some Useful Words

accident	*acidente*
bicycle	*bicicleta*
bus	*ônibus*
car	*carro* or *automóvel*
corner	*esquina*
highway	*estrada* or *caminho principal*
motorcycle	*motocicleta*
one-way street	*rua de mão única*
pedestrian	*pietão*
pedestrian/zebra crossing	*cruzamento*
street	*rua*
taxi	*taxi*
traffic	*trânsito*
traffic light	*sinal (de trânsito)*

| tram/streetcar | *bonde* |
| truck | *caminhão* |

Long-Distance Transport

Bus

For most Brazilians, buses are the only affordable form of long-distance transport. Bus services are generally excellent. The buses are clean and comfortable and the drivers are generally good.

In every big city, and most small ones, there is a main bus terminal known as a *rodoviária*. The *rodoviárias* are usually on the outskirts of the city.

There are two kinds of long-distance buses. The cheapest and most common is called a *comum*. It is reasonably comfortable and often has air-con and a toilet. The other kind of bus, the *leito* or *executiva*, is truly luxurious. It costs twice as much as a *comum*, but with fully reclining seats, blankets and pillows and, more often than not, a steward serving drinks, it is well worth the splurge for a longer journey.

Where is the bus station?
Onde é que fica a rodoviária?
What companies have buses to ....?
Quais são as companhias que tem ônibus para ....?
I want to go to .... by leito (comum).
Queiro ir para .... de leito (comum).
How much is the fare?
Quanto é a passagem?
What time does the bus leave?
A que horas sai o ônibus?

What time does the bus arrive in ....?
A que horas chega o ônibus em ....?
How long does the trip take?
Quanto tempo demora a viagem?
How many stops are there on the way?
Quantas paragens tem na via?

Air

VASP, Transbrasil, Rio-Sul and Cruzeiro are the major domestic carriers in Brazil. These airlines are supplemented by smaller domestic airlines, including *Nordeste, Taba, Votec* and *Tam*. There is also a fleet of air taxis which fly almost anywhere.

If you are lucky you can get a free flight with FAB (Força Aerea Brasileira). Go to the desk marked 'C.A.N.' in the airport and ask for the next military flight. Plane reservations can appear and disappear mysteriously. If you have a reservation it's often necessary to confirm it and reconfirm it, even if you've already bought the ticket.

When is the next flight to ....?
Quando sai o proximo voo para ....?
What time does the flight leave?
A que horas sai o voo?
I want to reserve a flight to ....
Queiro reservar um voo para ....
Which airlines fly to .... today (tomorrow)?
Quais são as aerolineas que voam para .... hoje (amanhã)?
How long does the flight take?
Quanto tempo demora o voo?

Will the flight leave on time?
  O voo sairá na hora?
Have they delayed the flight?
  Adiaram o voo?
How long has the flight been delayed?
  Quanto tempo foi adiado o voo?
I would like a one-way ticket to ....
  Queiro uma passagem de ida para ....
How much is a return ticket to ....?
  Quanto custa uma passagem de ida e volta para ....?
I have a 'Brazil Air Pass'.
  Tenho um 'Brasil Air Pass'.
Do you need my passport?
  Precisa do meu passaporte?

Local Transport
Local Bus
Local bus services tend to be pretty good in Brazil. Since most Brazilians take the bus to work everyday, municipal buses are usually frequent and their network of routes is comprehensive. They are also always cheap and crowded.

Does this bus go to ....?
  Este ônibus vai para ....?
What bus goes to?
  Qual é o ônibus que vai para ....?
How much is the fare?
  Quanto é a passagem?
Can you tell me when we get to ....?
  Me pode dizer quando chegamos a ....?
Excuse me, I want to get off the bus here.
  Com licença, queiro sair do ônibus aqui.

Taxis

The taxis in big cities tend to have meters which are updated by a *tabela* that converts the price on the meter to a new price – the inflation rate is so high that the meters cannot be updated fast enough. If the taxi doesn't have a meter, or it doesn't work, negotiate a fare before getting in.

Where can I find a taxi?
Onde é que posso encontrar um táxi?
Can you take me to ....?
Me pode levar para ....?
How much would it cost to go to ....?
Quanto custaria ir para ....?
That is too much.
É demais.
I need a táxi to go to the airport.
Preciso de um taxi para ir ao aeroporto.
How much do I owe you?
Quanto lhe devo?
Can you wait here for 10 minutes?
Pode esperar aqui dez minutos?

Car Rental

Renting a car is expensive; prices are comparable with those in the USA and Europe. Volkswagen bugs (called *fuscas* in Brazil) are the cheapest cars to rent.

Where can I rent a car?
Onde é que posso alugar um carro?
I would like to rent a car.
Queiro alugar um carro.

How much is the rental for one day (one week)?
Cuanto é o alugel para um dia (uma semana)?
Does that include mileage?
Isso incluye a kilometragem?
What kind of car do you have for hire?
Que tipo de carro tem para alugar?
Where can I buy some petrol?
Onde é que posso comprar gasolina?
How much does petrol cost?
Quanto custa a gasolina?
Do I need insurance?
Preciso de segurança?

Directions

east	*este*
north	*norte*
south	*sul*
west	*oeste*
left	*esquerda*
right	*direita*
straight ahead	*direito* or *em frente*

Instructions

Stop at the next corner please.
Pare na proxima esquina por favor.
Turn left (right) here.
Dobra a esquerda (direita) aqui.

Continue straight ahead.
  Sempre em frente. or *Sempre direito.*
Take the second side street on the right.
  Tome a segunda travessa a direita.

Around Town

Asking Directions

If you ask Brazilians to give you directions, it is almost certain that they will comply. The only problem is that people will often go out of their way to give an answer, even if they don't have the foggiest idea where your destination is. It pays to ask more than one person. Of course, if you end up with three sets of directions to the one place, you are no better off than when you started. A rule of thumb, followed by many long term foreign residents, is to keep asking until you get the same answer three times.

Could you tell me where .... is?	*Me pode dizer onde fica ....?*
Where is ....?	*Onde fica ....?*
the bank	*o banco*
the bus stop	*a paragem de ônibus*
the (Argentinian) consulate	*o consulado (argentino)*
the (Venezuelan) embassy	*a embaixada (venezolano)*
the market	*o mercado*
I am looking for	*Estou procurando .....*
my hotel	*o meu hotel*
the post office	*o correo*
the police station	*a delgacia*
the tourist office	*agência de turismo*

45

At the Bank

Changing money in Brazil can be a horrific experience. The banking system in most cities is extremely archaic, with computers being virtually unknown in all but the largest centres. In some of the smaller towns it can take over an hour to change a travellers' cheque, and even changing cash can be most frustrating. There is no easy way around this problem – patience and a big smile are the only answer – if you become impatient or, even worse, lose your temper you can expect your transaction time to double!

I want to change some money.
   Quero trocar dinheiro.
I want to change a/some travellers' cheque(s).
   Quero trocar um/algums cheque(s) de viagem.

Some Useful Words

bank	*banco*
black market	*mercado paralelo*
cashier/teller	*caixa*
commission	*comissão*
credit card	*carta de credito*
exchange rate	*curso de câmbio*
money (general)	*dinheiro*
coin	*moeda*
note	*nota*

Black Market

Changing money on the black market in Brazil is illegal. This of course doesn't stop anyone making black market transactions, but it is worth choosing your contact carefully. The exchange rate on the black market varies from 30% to

130% more than the official rate, depending on political tensions and the demand for hard currency, among other things.

To get an idea of what the US dollar is worth on the black market, just buy a copy of one of the major regional newspapers. The black market rate is generally printed alongside the official rate in the finance section of the paper. Of course this will only give you a rough idea. Travellers' cheques generally pay less than cash.

Do you know where I can change some dollars?
Sabe onde posso trocar algums dólares?
Will you change travellers' cheques?
Você troque cheques de viagem?
How much will you give me for each dollar?
Quanto é que você me da pra cada dólar?

At the Post Office

The Brazilian postal service is not much better than the banking system. Once you have written on it, there is never enough room left on a postcard for all the stamps needed to get the card out of the country. The stamps taste foul and don't stick very well. Where glue is supplied, it sticks to everything, so a visit to the post office often has to followed by a visit to the bathroom to wash your hands. As with the banks, impatience is rewarded with slower service.

I would like some stamps please.
Quero algums selos por favor.

I would like to send a letter/postcard/package to (Australia).
Quero mandar uma carta/um cartão postal/um pacote a (Australia).
I would like to send it registered mail please.
Quero manda-lo registrado por favor.
How much does it cost to send this to (England)?
Quanto custa mandar isto a (Inglaterrra)?

Some Useful Words

air mail	*correio aéreo*
poste restante	*poste restante*
surface mail	*via superfície*
telegram	*telegrama*

Telephone

Local calls in Brazil are very cheap. They can be made from public phones in the street or at telephone centres. Special coins (*fichas telefónicas*) are needed for this purpose, and can be bought from most street vendors or in telephone centres.

Long-distance calls within Brazil are reasonably priced considering the size of the country. Although it is possible to call long distance from some street phones, the *fichas* run out very quickly. International call tariffs are exorbitant. Many telephone centres are open 24 hours. The queues can be very long during the day, so it might be a good idea to wait until late evening to make your call.

I would like to speak with (Senhor Gonçalves).
Quero falar com o (Senhor Gonçalves).

Hello, is (Sandra) there?
Alo, a (Sandra) esta?
I would like to make a reverse charge (collect) call to (Canada).
Quero telefonar a cobrar a (Canada).
How much does it cost per minute?
Quanto custo o minuto?
What time is it in (California) now?
Que horas são em (California) agora?

Some Useful Words

engaged (occupied)	*ocupado*
public telephone	*orelhão*
telephone book	*lista telefónica*
telephone call	*telefonema*
telephone coin	*ficha telefónica*

Security

Personal security is a major concern for the traveller in Brazil. Unfortunately, with poverty as widespread as it is, theft is a common occurrence. Good advice for travellers is to leave any jewellery or expensive watches at home or, at the very least, in your hotel.

Violent crime is a very real problem in Brazil. Think twice before wandering into a *favela* (slum) alone. Also make sure that you always (and that means always) have some money on you. If someone does stick a gun in your face, the last thing you want to say is that you left all your money at the hotel.

If you must walk around alone at night in the big cities, try and stick to the well-lit areas. Walking down the middle of the road makes you a less likely target, as you are more visible. Women need to be doubly careful.

Leave me alone (in peace).	*Me deixa em paz.*
Don't bother me.	*Não amola.*
I've been robbed.	*Me roubaram.*
They took	*Levaram ....*
my money	*meu dinheiro*
my passport	*meu passaporte*

Some Useful Words

assault	*assalto*
Help!	*Socorro!*
insurance	*seguro*
knife	*faca*
pistol	*pistola*
thief	*ladrão*

Some Useful Phrases

What time does it open?
 A que horas abra?
What time does it close?
 A que horas fecha?
Where must I go to extend my visa?
 Para onde é que preciso ir para renovar men visto?
I would like to extend my visa.
 Quero renovar meu visto.

In the Country

beach	*praia*
city	*cidade*
farm	*finca*
hill	*monte*
hinterland/bush	*sertão*
jungle	*selva*
mountain	*montanha*
ocean	*oceano*
plain	*planície*
river	*rio*
swamp/marsh/wetlands	*pantanal*
village	*aldeia* or *povo* (smaller)

Weather

Boy it's hot today! (a common complaint from taxi drivers)
  Come é quente hoje! or somewhat stronger *Que calor danado!*
The wind is very strong.
  O vento é bem forte.
It's raining.
  Está chovendo.
Are you hot (cold)?
  Está com calor (frio)?
I'm hot (cold).
  Estou com calor (frio).
The sun is very strong.
  O sol é bem forte.

51

Some Useful Words

cloud	*nuvem*
rain	*chuva*
rainbow	*arco-íris*
snow	*neve*
storm	*tempestade*
sun	*sol*
weather	*tempo*
wind	*vento*

Animals

animal	*animal*
bird	*ave*
butterfly	*borboleta*
cat	*gato*
chicken	*galinha*
cow	*vaca*
dog	*cão*
fish	*peixe*
fly	*mosca*
lizard	*lagarto*
mosquito	*mosquito*
ox	*boi*
pig	*porco*
sheep	*carneiro*
snake	*serpente*
spider	*aranha*

Plants

breadfruit tree	*jaqueira*
cactus	*cacto*
carnation	*cravo*

coconut palm	*coqueiro*
daisy	*margarida*
flower	*flor*
guava tree	*goiabeira*
mango tree	*mangueira*
palm tree	*palmeira*
pine	*pinho*
rose	*rosa*
sugar cane	*canha de açucar*
tree	*árvore*

Food

The average Brazilian lives on beans (*feijão*), rice (*arroz*)
and noodles (*macarrão*). Once in a while they can afford to
add some meat (*carne*) to that concoction, but that is
certainly a luxury for most. The cheapest meat is chicken
(*frango*), but pork (*carne de cerdo*) is also a fairly common
staple for those with a little extra to spend. There is plenty of
Beef (*carne de boi*) in Brazil.

Brazilian Meals

Feijoada – could almost be considered the national dish. It is
a bean-based meal with odd bits of meat (mainly pork,
sausage, and sometimes beef) and various other
ingredients. It is always served with rice and *farofa*, which
is manioc flower fried with onion and egg. Beyond that
there is no hard and fast recipe; rather it contains
whatever the family can afford. It can be fairly stodgy, and
very spicy. No trip to Brazil is complete without trying this
at least once and it's very likely that you will eat it on
numerous occasions.

Sarapatel – a definite favourite among Brazilians, though it
is certainly not to every foreigner's liking. It is basically a
mixture of pork giblets, pork lard, blood, mint leaf and an
assortment of spices.

Acarajé – another bean-based dish with salt, onions, palm
oil and peppers. It also often contains shrimps.

Moqueca – a seafood stew which can contain a variety of
seafoods such as lobster, octopus, squid, oyster,

crab, or whatever fish came in on the fishing boat that morning. It is heavily flavoured with tomato, onion, coriander, some kind of citrus fruit juice, salt (of course), and Brazil's favourite – coconut milk.

Vatapá – consists of shrimp, herring and cashew nuts, with a garlic, pepper, coconut milk, and palm oil sauce. Delicious!

Xinxim de galinha – chicken and shrimp in an onion, garlic, citrus, palm oil and salt and pepper sauce.

Sururú – a very tasty mussel dish.

Carne de sol – a very salty meat; definitely not for anyone with hardening arteries. It is generally grilled and served with an assortment of beans, rice and vegies. The closest thing I know of in the west is beef jerky.

Siri – stuffed crab. You can often find this in beachfront restaurants.

Agulha – a very thin fish that looks a little like a garfish. It is barbecued and, if you're lucky, brought to you on the beach. You eat the entire thing, head, bones and all. It is definitely more of a snack than a full meal, but of course if you ate enough. . .

Tapioca – found mainly in the north and, especially, north-east. It is the Brazilian equivalent of a taco. Basically it is a manioc-flower pancake which is cooked over an open fire in a frying pan. The most likely place to find it is in markets or somewhere outside where the locals hang out in the evening. As a delicious option you might ask for it with cheese (*com quiejo*), in which case it is fried with an enormous lump of fresh goat's cheese in the middle.

Churrasco – basically barbecued meat, especially beef. The best places to try it are called *churrasquerias*.

Meat

beef	*carne de boi*
chicken	*frango* or *galinha*
mutton	*carne de carneiro*
pork	*carne de cerdo*

Seafood

fish	*peixe*
fried fish	*peixe frito*
grilled fish	*peixe grelhado*
cod	*bacalhau*
crab	*carangueijo*
lobster	*lagosta*
oyster	*ostra*
shellfish	*marisco*
trout	*truta*

Fruit

The incredible diversity of fruits in Brazil never ceases to amaze the visitor. Almost the entire country is in the tropics, so tropical fruits are certainly the most abundant. However, in the region south of São Paulo, there are huge orchards full of the temperate fruits that you find all over the USA, Australia and Europe. Some fruit found only in the northern regions will send your tastebuds into a frenzy.

fruit	*fruta*
apple	*maçã*
apricot	*damasco*

avocado	*aguacate*
banana	*banana* or *plátano*
breadfruit	*fruta de pão*
coconut	*côco*
grape	*uva*
guava	*goiaba*
honeydew melon	*melão*
lemon	*limão*
mango	*manga*
orange	*laranja*
papaya	*mamão*
peach	*pêssego*
pear	*pera*
pineapple	*abacaxí*
plum, prune	*ameixa*
strawberry	*morango*
tangerine	*tangerina*
tomato	*tomate*
watermelon	*melancia*

Other Fruits

Bacaba – a fruit found in the Amazon; it is used to make wines and syrups.

Biribá – another Amazonian fruit, which is eaten plain.

Cacao – produces the seeds from which chocolate is made. The fruit is also good.

Cajú – looks like a red or yellow pepper with a kidney on top. The 'kidney' is roasted then split open to reveal a single cashew nut. The fruit makes a wonderful juice when mixed with a little sugar. Some people like to eat the fruit plain.

Fruto do conde – a very popular sweet fruit from the apple family.
Graviola – a large fruit with a bumpy green skin and yellow flesh. It makes a delicious ice cream.
Jaca – jackfruit. It also makes a great ice cream.

Vegetables

bean	*feijão*
carrot	*cenoura*
cauliflower	*coliflor*
corn	*milho*
cucumber	*pepino*
garlic	*alho*
lettuce	*alface*
mushroom	*cogumelo*
onion	*cebola*
pumpkin	*abóbora*
vegetable	*vegetal*

Eggs

egg	*ovo*
fried egg	*ovo frito*
boiled egg	*ovo cozido*
scrambled eggs	*ovos mexidos*
poached eggs	*ovos escalfados*

Dairy Products

butter	*mantega*
cheese	*queijo*
goat's cheese	*queijo de cabra*
milk	*leite*
yoghurt	*iogurte*

Bread & Sweets

bread	*pão*
sweet bread	*pão doce*
toast	*pão tostado*

Many sweets can be bought over the counter in bakeries (*paderias*). The variety can be a bit daunting, but most people seem to get what they want simply by pointing.

cake	*torta*
ice cream	*gelado*
sweet	*doce*

Brazilian ice creams are a delight. In the best ice cream parlours (*geladerias*), you might find up to 50 different flavours. Most of them are made from tropical fruit and are often distinctly Brazilian.

Sweeteners

honey	*mel*
sugar	*açucar*

Condiments

chilli sauce	*salsa picante*
mustard	*mostarda*
pepper	*pimenta*
salt	*sal*
vinegar	*vinagre*

Drinks
Alcoholic

Brazilian beers are pretty good. The national favourites are

Cerva, Antartica and Brahma Chopp (pronounced 'shopee').

beer	*cerveja*

Brazilian wines are not very good. You can get some good imported wines if you want to splurge. Portuguese or Chilean wines offer the best value for money.

white wine	*vinho branco*
red wine	*vinho tinto*

When Brazilians want to get rolling drunk without spending too much, they drink *cachaça* (also known as *pinga* or *aguardente*). It is a very high-proof, sugar-cane alcohol. You need an asbestos stomach to drink any real quantities of this stuff straight. Still, it makes for a really potent mixer and is certainly much more palatable that way.

Non-Alcoholic

Coffee is another not to be missed experience in Brazil. Most people drink it very strong and very sweet, so if you want it some other way you'll have to make it very clear. Very often if you say *sem açucar* (without sugar), they won't believe what they heard and will assume that you asked for extra sugar. If you say nothing you will certainly get sugar.

coffee (small, strong and sweet)	*cafezinho*
black coffee (probably with sugar)	*café negro*
white coffee (made with milk)	*café com leite*
white coffee (with milk added)	*café com leite frio*
instant coffee	*nescafé*

milk	*leite*
mineral water	*agua mineral*
with gas	*com gas*
without gas	*sem gas*
tea	*chá*
water	*agua*

In Brazil you will find all the soft drinks that you know so well back home – Coke, 7-UP, Fanta (there is also strawberry Fanta). Undoubtedly the king of soft-drinks in Brazil, however, is *guaraná*. There are a few companies that make this drink, but the best are Brahma and Antartica. Look out for these.

You can also buy *guaraná em pô* (powdered *guaraná*), which you mix up like a cordial, adding sugar to taste. It is said to be very high in vitamins. It is made from an Amazonian berry, and can be found all over the country.

In a Restaurant
One thing you will notice about Brazil is the variety of eating establishments. Chinese restaurants are very popular and can be very cheap. Seafood restaurants can also be reasonably priced.

Could I see the menu please?
  Posso ver a carta por favor?
I would like the soup of the day please.
  Queiro a sopa do dia por favor.
I am a vegetarian.
  Sou vegetário.
I cannot eat meat.
  Não posso comer carne.

Not too spicy please.
   Não muito picante por favor.
Could you please bring some salt and pepper?
   Pode trazer sal e pimento por favor?
Could you bring the bill please?
   Pode trazer a conta por favor?

Shopping

Bargaining

Bargaining is pretty much the standard way of doing any small business transaction in Brazil. The most common place for this kind of transaction is either in a market or in a small shop. In department stores or food shops bargaining will get you nowhere.

How much does this cost?
Quanto custa isso?
It costs 10,000 cruzados.
Custa dez mil cruzados.
That is very expensive.
É muito caro.
That is too expensive for me.
Isso é caro demais para mim.
That is highway robbery!
Isso é um roubo!
I found it cheaper in another shop.
O encontrei mais barato numa outra loja.
Can you bring the price down a little?
Pode baixar o preço um pouquinho?
I will give you 5000 cruzados.
Lhe dou cinco mil cruzados.
Not one cruzado more!
Nem mais um cruzado!

Clothing

Clothing in Brazil can vary quite considerably in quality.

Like anywhere else, if you buy the cheapest clothes on the market in Brazil they invariably fall apart before too long. Brazil is the world's largest wholesale manufacturer of shoes but, unless you have changed your money on the black market, you will not find them particularly cheap.

bathing suit	*roupa de banho*
bikini	*bikini*
coat	*paletó*
dress	*vestido*
hat	*chapeu*
jacket	*casaco*
pullover	*pullover*
sandals	*sandálias*
shirt	*camisa*
shoes	*sapatos*
shorts	*calções*
skirt	*saia*
socks	*peúgas*
tights	*malha*
trousers	*calças*
underpants	*calçãozinho*
underwear	*roupa interior*

Brazilian beaches (particularly Copacabana and Ipanema) are famous for a daring bikini known as *fio dental*. The name means 'dental floss'; I'll leave the rest to your imagination.

Stationery

exercise book	*caderno*
guide book	*guia*
magazine	*revista*

map	*mapa*
newspaper	*jornal*
note book	*agenda*
novel	*romance*
pen	*caneta*
pencil	*lápis*
writing paper	*papel de escrever*

Colours

black	*negro/a*
blue	*azul*
brown	*marrom* or *cor castanha*
green	*verde*
orange	*cor laranja*
pink	*rosa*
purple	*púrpura*
red	*vermelho* or *tinto*
white	*branco/a*
yellow	*amarelo/a*

Weights & Measures

The metric system is fairly universal in Brazil, although cheese is often measured in pounds (*libras*)!

centimetre	*centímetro*
metre	*metro*
kilometre	*kilómetro*
gram	*grama*
kilogram	*kiló*

Size & Comparison

big	*grande*
bigger	*maior*
biggest	*o maior*
small	*pequeno*
smaller	*menor*
smallest	*o menor*
heavy	*pesado*
heavier	*mais pesado*
light	*ligero*
lighter	*mais ligero* or *menos pesado*
long	*comprido*
tall	*alto*
short	*breve* (in stature – *baixo*)
few	*poucos*
some	*algums/algumas*
much	*muito*
many	*muitos*
thin	*magro*
thick	*grosso*
fat	*gordo*
fast	*rápido*
slow	*devagar*

Some Useful Phrases

I would like to buy ....
    Queiro comprar ....
Do you have this in another colour?
    Tem isso num outro cor?
Don't you have a cheaper one?
    Não tem mais barato?

I'm just looking.
Estou olhando só.
It is too big (too small) for me.
É grande demais (pequeno demais) para mim.
Could you wrap it please?
Pode embalar-lo por favor?
Do you have a bag?
Tem uma bolsa?
I want that one please.
Quiero aquilo por favor.
Could you show me another one?
Me pode mostrar outro?
Where can I find ....?
Onde posso encontrar ....?
Do you have books in English?
Tem livros em inglés?

Some Useful Words

brush	*escouva*
button	*botão*
comb	*pente*
department store	*armazém*
market	*mercado*
needle	*agulha*
shop	*loja*
soap	*sabonete*
thread	*fio*
toilet paper	*papel higénico*
toothbrush	*escova de dentes*
toothpaste	*creme dentífrico*

Health

If you can avoid it, don't get sick in Brazil. It's not that there aren't good doctors or hospitals around, it's just that it might be difficult to find them unless you have connections in the know. Some hospitals have a reputation among Brazilians as death traps, so it is worth asking around before deciding to visit any.

Of course, if you do need to see a doctor, you will need to be able to tell him/her what your problem is.

I need a doctor.
Preciso de um médico.
Where can I find a good doctor?
Onde posso encontrar um bom médico?
Is there a hospital near here?
Tem por aquí um hospital?
I am ill.
Estou doente.
My friend (female) is ill.
Minha amiga está doente.
My friend (male) is ill.
Meu amigo está doente.
Could you please call a doctor?
Você pode chamar um médico por favor?
I need a dentist.
Preciso de um dentista.

Complaints
allergy   *alergia*

68

anaemia	*anemia*
asthma	*asma*
burn	*queimadura*
constipation	*prisão de ventre*
cough	*toso*
cramp	*cãibra*
diarrhoea	*diarreia*
dysentery	*disenteria*
fever	*febre*
headache	*dor de cabeça*
infection	*infecção*
itch	*sarna*
malaria	*malária*
pain	*dor*
rash	*erupção na pele*
stomachache	*dor de barriga*
sunburn	*quiemadura do sol*
sunstroke	*insolação*
toothache	*dor de dentes*
yellow fever	*febre amarelo*

Parts of the Body

arm	*braço*
back	*costas*
blood	*sangue*
bone	*osso*
chest	*peito*
ear	*orelha*
eye	*olho*
foot	*pé*
hand	*mão*
head	*cabeça*

heart	*coração*
knee	*joelho*
leg	*perna*
mouth	*boca*
nose	*naríz*
shoulder	*ombro*
stomach	*barriga* or *estómago*
teeth	*dentes*
throat	*garganta*

At the Chemist

Many drugs which require a prescription in the developed world can be bought over the counter in any pharmacy in Brazil. Generic names for various pharmaceuticals can vary from one country to another, so be aware of what it is that you are buying. Also check the use-by date: Brazil's climate causes things to go off rather quickly.

Another problem is that many international drug companies test their new products in Brazil (among other countries) before deciding whether or not to release them in the developed world.

I need something for a runny nose.
  Preciso algo para a costipação.
Do you have sun-tan lotion?
  Tem bronceador?
Do I need a prescription for ....?
  Preciso de uma receita para ....?

Some Useful Words

antibiotics	*antibióticos*
antiseptic	*anti-séptico*

aspirin	*aspirinas*
bandage	*ligadura*
contraceptive	*anticonceptivo*
injection	*injecção*
paracetamol	*paracétamol*
tablet	*comprimido*
tampon	*tampão*

Some Useful Words

accident	*accidente*
blood test	*análise de sangue*
broken	*roto*
faeces	*fezes*
injury	*ferimento*
nurse	*enfermeira*
urine	*urina*
wound	*ferida*

Time & Dates

Days

Monday	*segunda-feira*
Tuesday	*terça-feira*
Wednesday	*quarta-feira*
Thursday	*quinta-feira*
Friday	*sexta-feira*
Saturday	*sabado*
Sunday	*domingo*

Months

January	*janeiro*
February	*fevereiro*
March	*março*
April	*avril*
May	*maio*
June	*junho*
July	*julho*
August	*agosto*
September	*setembro*
October	*otubro*
November	*novembro*
December	*dizembro*

Dates

What date is it?	*Que data é?*

It is ....   *É a ....*
     30 March   *trinta de março*
     Monday 21 July   *segunda feira vinte e um de*
                              julho

Present, Past & Future

Present

now	*agora*
today	*hoje*
tonight	*hoje de noite*
this morning	*hoje de manhã*
this week	*este semana*
this year	*este ano*
this month	*este mes*

Past

yesterday	*ontem*
the day before yesterday	*a dois dias atras*
a few days ago	*faz alguns dias*
yesterday morning	*ontem de manhã*
yesterday evening	*ontem de tarde*
last week	*a semana passada*
last month	*o mes passado*
last year	*o ano passado*
just before	*faz poco tempo*
quite a while ago	*faz bastante tempo*
long ago	*faz muito tempo*

Future

tomorrow	*amanhã*

day after tomorrow	*daqui a dois dias*
tomorrow evening	*amanhã de tarde*
tomorrow morning	*amanhã de manhã*
next week	*a semana que vem*
next month	*o mes que vem*
next year	*o ano que vem*
later	*depois*

Some Useful Words

day	*dia*
night	*noite*
morning	*manhã*
evening	*tarde*
week	*semana*
month	*mes*
year	*ano*
not yet	*ainda não*
everyday	*todos os dias*
always	*sempre*

Time

The word *horas*, meaning 'hours', is instrumental in telling the time.

What time is it?	*Que horas são?*

There are two possible ways to answer this question. If it is any hour other than 1 o'clock, whether am or pm, the answer uses a plural form of the verb *ser*. Otherwise the singular form is used. Rather than dividing the day into am and pm, in Portuguese you say *da tarde* (of the afternoon) from midday until sunset, *da noite* (of the night) from sunset until midnight, and *da manhã* (of the morning) from midnight until midday.

It is	*É* ....
1 pm	*uma hora da tarde*
1 am	*uma hora da manhã*
midnight	*meia noite*
midday	*meio dia*

It is	*São* ....
7 am	*sete horas da manhã*
2 pm	*duas horas da tarde*
11 pm	*onze horas da noite*

6.25 am	*seis horas e vinte e cinco da manhã*
3.30 pm	*tres horas e meia da tarde*
8.15 pm	*oito horas e quinze da noite*
9.40 pm	*nove horas e quarenta da noite*

Sometimes the 24-hour clock is used, in which case it is not necessary to use *da manhã*, *da tarde* or *da noite*. See the Numbers chapter for all the remaining numbers that can be used for telling the time.

Numbers

Cardinal Numbers

0	*zero*
1	*um* (masculine)
	uma (feminine)
2	*dois* (masculine)
	duas (feminine)
3	*três*
4	*quatro*
5	*cinco*
6	*seis*
7	*sete*
8	*oito*
9	*nove*
10	*dez*
11	*onze*
12	*doze*
13	*treze*
14	*catorze*
15	*quinze*
16	*dezesseis*
17	*dezessete*
18	*dezoito*
19	*dezenove*
20	*vinte*
21	*vinte e um*
22	*vinte e dois*
23	*vinte e três*
30	*trinta*

31	*trinta e um*
40	*quarenta*
50	*cinquenta*
60	*sessenta*
70	*setenta*
80	*oitenta*
90	*noventa*
100	*cem*
101	*cento e um*
115	*cento e quinze*
146	*cento e quarenta e seis*
200	*duzentos*
300	*trezentos*
400	*quatrocentos*
500	*quinhentos*
600	*seiscentos*
700	*setecentos*
800	*oitocentos*
900	*novecentos*
1000	*mil*
2000	*dois mil*
3568	*três mil quinhentos e sessenta e oito*
100,000	*cem mil*
500,000	*quinhentos mil*
1,000,000	*um milhão*

one-quarter – ¼	*quarto*
one-third – ⅓	*terço*
one-half – ½	*meio*
1½	*um e meio*

Ordinal Numbers

The ordinal forms given in the following list are all
masculine. When the objects being counted are feminine,
the final *o* should be replaced with an *a*.

first	*primeiro*
second	*segundo*
third	*terçeiro*
fourth	*quarto*
fifth	*quinto*
sixth	*sexto*
seventh	*sétimo*
eighth	*oitavo*
ninth	*nono*
tenth	*décimo*
eleventh	*décimo primeiro*
twelth	*décimo segundo*
twentieth	*vigésimo*
twenty-fourth	*vigésimo quarto*
thirtieth	*trigésimo*

Money

Where the USA has its nickels, dimes and quarters, Brazil
has its *pau* or *barão*, both 1000 *cruzados*, and *duro*, which is
5000 *cruzados*. Thus *cinco duros* is the same as 25,000
cruzados.

Some Useful Words

count	*contar*
number	*número*
few	*pocos*
many	*muitos*

some	*algums/algumas*
how many?	*quantos?*
how much?	*quanto?* or *quanto é?*
too much	*demais*
enough	*bastante*

Vocabulary

A
able – *capaz*
accept – *aceitar*
accident – *acidente*
actor – *actor*
actress – *actriz*
address – *endereço*
aeroplane – *avião*
afraid – *com medo*
airport – *aeroporto*
aspirin – *aspirina*
aunt – *tia*

B
baby – *bebé*
bad – *mau*
bag – *bolsa*
bank – *banco*
because – *porque*
bicycle – *bicycleta*
birthday – *aniversário*
blood – *sangue*
book – *livro*
boy – *moço* or *rapaz*
boyfriend – *namorado*
bring – *trazer*
broke (without money) – *liso*
brush – *escova*

burn (n) – *queimadura*
burn (v) – *queimar*
busy (telephone) – *ocupado*
buy – *comprar*

C

camera – *máquina fotográfica*
candle – *vela*
car – *carro*
centre – *centro*
cheap – *barato*
chemist – *farmácia*
child – *criança*
choose – *escolher*
Christmas – *natal*
church – *igreja*
cinema – *cinema*
city – *cidada*
clean – *limpo*
clothing – *ropa*
c/o (care of) – *ao cuidado de*
collect (reverse charges) – *a cobrar*
congratulations – *parabéms*
cook – *cozinhar*
country – *pais* (eg Australia), *campo* (ie rural area)
couple – *par*
cry – *chorar*
cycle – *andar de bicicleta*

D

daily – *diario*
damage – *dano*

dance – *bailar*
dark – *oscuro*
darling – *querido/a*
date – *data*
daughter – *filha*
dawn – *madrugada*
day – *dia*
dead – *morto*
debt – *dívida*
decide – *decidir*
deep – *fundo*
delay – *adiar*
demand – *exigir*
dentist – *dentista*
depart – *partir*
describe – *describir*
develop – *revelar*
diamond – *diamante*
dinner – *jantar*
dirty – *sujo*
disagree – *não concordar*
disease – *doença*
dizzy – *vertigonoso*
doctor – *médico/a*
dog – *cão*
doll – *boneca*
door – *porta*
dormitory – *dormitório*
down(ward) – *para baixo*
dream – *sonho*
dress – *vestida*
drive – *dirigir*

drum – *tambor*
drunk – *bêbado*
dry – *seco*

E
each – *cada*
early – *cedo*
earn – *ganhar*
easy – *fácil*
Easter – *pasquas*
eat – *comer*
edge – *bordo*
election – *eleição*
electricity – *electicidade*
electrocute – *electrocutar*
elevator/lift – *elevador*
embassy – *embaixada*
emerald – *esmeralda*
employee – *empregado/a*
employer – *patrão*
empty – *vazio*
end – *fim*
engaged (telephone) – *ocupado*
enjoy – *gozar (de)*
enough – *bastante* or *suficiente*
envelope – *sobre*
every – *cada*
everybody – *todos*
everything – *tudo*
except – *salvo*
exit – *saida*
eye – *olho*

F

face – *rosto*
faint – *desmaiar*
faithful – *fiel*
family – *família*
fan – *ventilador*
far – *longe*
fare – *passagem*
farm – *fazenda*
fast – *rápido*
father – *pai*
fence – *barreira*
festival – *festa*
fever – *febre*
fiancé – *noivo*
fiancée – *noiva*
fight – *luta*
film (photographic) – *película*
fine (penalty) – *multa*
finger – *dedo*
fire – *fogo*
flavour – *sabor*
flower – *flor*
flu – *gripe*
food – *comida*
foreigner – *estrangeiro*
forget – *esquecer*
fork – *garfo*
fresh – *fresco/a*
friend – *amigo/a*
fruit – *fruta*
full – *cheio*

funny – *engraçado*
furniture – *móveis*

G

game – *jogo*
gaol – *prisão*
garbage – *lixo*
garden – *jardim*
garlic – *alho*
gate – *portão*
gem – *jóia*
girl – *moça*
girlfriend – *namorada*
give – *dar*
glove – *luva*
glue – *cola*
go – *ir*
goal – *gol*
goalkeeper – *guarda-redes*
God – *deus*
gold – *oro*
good – *bom* or *boa*
government – *governo*
grandchild – *neto*
grandparent – *avó*
grill – *grelhar*
guard – *guarda*
guitar – *violão*

H

hair – *cabelo*
hairdresser – *cabelereiro/a*

happen – *acontecer*
happy – *feliz*
hate – *odiar*
have – *ter*
head – *cabeça*
health (also 'cheers' when drinking) – *saúde*
hear – *ouvir*
heavy – *pesado*
help! – *socorro!*
here – *aqui*
hiccups – *soluços*
hill – *monte*
hitchhike – *andar de autostop*
holiday – *ferias*
honest – *honesto/a*
hope – *esperar*
house – *casa*
humid – *húmido*
hungry – *com fôme*
hunt – *caçar*
husband – *marido*

I

ice – *gelo*
ice cream – *gelado*
ill – *doente*
illegal – *ilegal*
immediately – *imediatamente*
inch – *polegada*
increase – *aumentar*
injection – *injecão*
injury – *ferida*

ink – *tinto*
insect – *insecto*
insurance – *seguros*
iodine – *íodo*
iron (clothes) – *passar*

J

jealous – *ciumento*
jewel – *joia*
job – *trabalho*
joke – *brincadera*
juice – *suco*

K

keep – *guardar*
key – *chave*
kick (football) – *chutar*
kill – *matar*
kitchen – *cozinha*
knife – *faca*
knock (on the door) – *bater (na porta)*
know (something) – *saber*
know (someone) – *conocer*

L

lake – *lago*
lamp – *lámapada*
landslide – *desmoronamento (de terra)*
language – *língua*
last – *último*
late – *tarde*
laugh – *rir*

laundry – *lavanderia*
law – *lei*
lazy – *preguiçoso*
leaf – *folha*
letter – *carta*
lid – *tampa*
life – *vida*
like (v) – *gostar de*
live (to inhabit) – *morar*
lock – *fechar a chave*
look – *olhar*
lose – *perder*
lost – *perdido*
love – *amar* or *querer*
lunch – *almoço*

M

machine – *máquina*
magazine – *revista*
mail – *correio*
make – *fazer*
make-up – *maquilhagem*
man – *homem*
manager – *direitor*
married – *casado*
marry – *casar*
match (for lighting) – *fósforo*
mattress – *colchão*
meat – *carne*
medicine – *medicina*
mend – *consertar*
menu – *menú* or *cardápio*

milk – *leite*
mirror – *espelho*
mistake – *erro*
money – *dinhero*
more – *mais*
mother – *mãe*
mouse – *rato*
moustache – *bigode*
move – *mover*

N

near – *perto de*
nearly – *quase*
necklace – *colar*
nephew – *sobrinho*
never – *nunca* or *jamais*
new – *novo/a*
news – *notícias*
next – *o próximo*
nice – *simpático*
niece – *sobrinha*
no – *não*
nose – *nariz*
nothing – *nada*
now – *agora*

O

octopus – *polvo*
offend – *ofender*
offer – *oferecer*
office – *escritorio*
official – *oficial*

often – *muitas vezes* or *com frequencia*
oil – *óleo*
old – *velho/a*
olive – *azeitona*
only – *só* or *somente*
open – *aberto*
operation – *operação*
opportunity – *oportunidade*
or – *ou*
orphan – *orfão/orfã*
outside – *fora*
oven – *forno*
owe – *dever*

P

packet – *pacote*
page – *página*
pain – *dor*
paint – *tinta*
painting – *quadra*
pale – *pálido/a*
pants – *calções*
paper – *papel*
parade – *desfile*
parcel – *embalagem*
parents – *paes*
party – *festa*
passenger – *passageiro/a*
path – *cominho*
patient – *paciente*
pay – *pagar*
pedestrian – *pietão*

pen – *caneta*
people – *gente*
pepper – *pimenta*
perhaps – *tal vez*
person – *pessoa*
petrol – *gasolina*
place – *lugar*
plan – *plano*
plate – *prato*
pocket – *bolsa*
poor – *pobre*
pregnant – *grávida*
prisoner – *prisoneiro*
probably – *provavelmente*
profit – *prófito*
pub – *cervejaria*
purse – *porta-moedas*
pyjamas – *pijama*

Q

question – *pergunta*
quickly – *rapidamente*
quiet – *tranquilo*

R

rabbit – *coelho*
railway – *estrada de ferro*
rain – *chuva*
rape – *violar*
raw – *cru*
read – *ler*
ready – *pronto*

reason – *razão*
receipt – *recibo*
reef – *recife*
remember – *lembrar*
restaurant – *restaurante*
rich – *rico*
ring – *anel*
ripe – *maduro*
risk – *risco*
river – *rio*
roast – *assar*
rob – *roubar*
robber – *ladrão*
robbery – *roubo*
rubbish – *lixo*
rude – *mal educado*
run – *correr*

S
sad – *triste*
salad – *ensalada*
same – *mesmo*
sand – *arreia*
sauce – *molho*
say – *dizer*
scenery – *paissagem*
school – *escola*
scratch – *aranhadura*
sea – *mar*
season – *estação*
seat – *silha*
see – *ver*

send – *mandar*
servant – *criado/a*
sew – *coser*
shade – *sombra*
sheep – *ovelha*
shellfish – *marisco*
ship – *navío* or *barco*
shop – *loja*
shut – *fechar*
side – *lado*
silver – *plata*
simple – *fácil*
sit – *sentar*
size – *tamanho*
sleep – *dormir*
slowly – *devagar*
small – *pequeno*
smoke – *fumar*
soap – *sabonete*
song – *canção*
soon – *logo*
sound – *som*
souvenir – *lembrança*
speak – *falar*
spoon – *colher*
sport – *esporte*
star – *estrela*
stay – *ficar*
steal – *roubar*
street – *rua*
strong – *forte*

sugar – *açucar*
sweet – *doce*

T

table – *mesa*
tablet – *comprimido*
take – *tomar*
tanned (by sun) – *bronceado*
taste – *gosto*
tea – *chá*
thankyou – *obrigado/a*
then (at that time) – *então*
thief – *ladrão*
think – *pensar*
threaten – *ameaçar*
ticket – *bilhete*
toilet – *retrete*
tomorrow – *amanhã*
tonight – *hoje de noite*
touch – *tocar*
traffic – *trânsito*
train – *trem*
translate – *traduzir*
travel – *viajar*
truck – *caminhão*
typewriter – *máquina de escrever*

U

ugly – *feio/a*
umbrella – *guarda-chuva*
uncle – *tio*
under – *em baixo de*

understand – *entender* or *compreender*
unless – *a não ser que*
unpack – *desfazer (as malas)*
unripe – *verde*
untidy – *desarrumado*
until – *até que*
up – *para cima*
useful – *útil*

V

vacancy – *vaga*
vegetable – *vegetal*
vegetarian – *vegetariano*
very – *muito/a*
via – *por*
view – *vista*
visa – *visto*
visit – *visitar*
vomit – *vomitar*
voyage – *viagem*

W

wage – *salário*
wait – *esperar*
walk – *andar*
wallet – *carteira*
want – *querer*
war – *guerra*
wardrobe – *guarda-roupa*
wash – *lavar*
watch (time) – *relógio*
water – *água*

waterfall – *catarata*
week – *semana*
wet – *molhado*
wife – *mulher*
window – *janela*
wood – *madeira*
wool – *lã*
work – *trabalhar*
wrap – *embalar*
write – *escrever*

X

x-rays – *raios-x* (pronounced as 'sheesh')

Y

yacht – *iate*
yam – *inhame*
year – *ano*
yes – *sim*
yesterday – *ontem*
young – *jovem*

Z

zoo – *jardim zoológico*

98 Notes

Language survival kits

Burmese phrasebook
Burmese will help travellers make the most of the limited time they are allowed to spend in Burma.

China phrasebook
Covers China's official language, Mandarin (*Putonghua*), with *pinyin* spellings & Chinese characters.

Hindi/Urdu phrasebook
Hindi and Urdu are closely related languages that are spoken in north India and Pakistan.

Indonesia phrasebook
A little Indonesian is easy to learn, and it's almost identical to Malay so this book is doubly useful.

Japanese phrasebook
Essential vocabulary and phrases to help travellers discover Japan. Japanese script throughout.

Korean phrasebook
This book is designed for independent travellers, and Korean script is given throughout.

Nepali phrasebook
Nepali is spoken in parts of India, Sikkim and Bhutan as well as Nepal. This book includes a special trekking chapter.

Papua New Guinea phrasebook
Pidgin is PNG's lingua franca, also spoken with minor variations in the Solomon Islands and Vanuatu.

Pilipino phrasebook
Pilipino, also known as Tagalog, is the Philippines' national language and is spoken by almost half the population.

Quechua phrasebook
Quechua (Runasimi), the language of the Incas, is still spoken widely in rural Peru and Bolivia.

Sri Lanka phrasebook
This book covers Sinhala, Sri Lanka's national language, and is designed for people who want to get off the beaten track.

Swahili phrasebook
Swahili is widely spoken throughout East Africa – from the coast of Kenya and Tanzania through to Zaïre.

Thai phrasebook
This book uses easy-to-follow pronunciation symbols and also includes Thai script.

Tibet phrasebook
Tibetan is spoken in a number of Chinese provinces, Nepal, Sikkim and Ladakh. Tibetan script is included for all phrases.

Travel Survival Kits

Alaska
Argentina
Australia
Baja California
Bali & Lombok
Bangladesh
Bolivia
Brazil
Burma
Canada
Central Africa
Chile & Easter Island
China
Colombia
East Africa
Ecuador & the Galapagos Islands
Egypt & the Sudan
Fiji
Hong Kong, Macau & Canton
India
Indonesia
Israel
Japan
Jordan & Syria
Karakoram Highway
Kashmir, Ladakh & Zanskar
Kathmandu & the Kingdom of Nepal
Korea
Madagascar & the Comoros
Malaysia, Singapore & Brunei
Maldives & Is. of the East Indian Ocean
Mauritius, Réunion & the Seychelles
Mexico
Micronesia
Morocco, Algeria & Tunisia
New Zealand
Pakistan
Papua New Guinea
Peru
Philippines
Raratonga & the Cook Islands
Samoa
Solomon Islands
Sri Lanka

Tahiti & French Polynesia
Taiwan
Thailand
Tibet
Tonga
Turkey
West Africa
Yemen

Shoestring Guides

Africa on a shoestring
Eastern Europe on a shoestring
North-East Asia on a shoestring
South America on a shoestring
South-East Asia on a shoestring
West Asia on a shoestring

Trekking & Walking Guides

Bushwalking in Australia
Tramping in New Zealand
Trekking in the Indian Himalaya
Trekking in the Nepal Himalaya
Trekking in Turkey

Phrasebooks

Burmese phrasebook
Brazilian phrasebook
China phrasebook
Hindi/Urdu phrasebook
Indonesia phrasebook
Japanese phrasebook
Korean phrasebook
Nepal phrasebook
Papua New Guinea phrasebook
Pilipino phrasebook
Quechua phrasebook
Sri Lanka phrasebook
Swahili phrasebook
Thai phrasebook
Tibet phrasebook

And Also

Travel with Children
Travellers Tales

Lonely Planet travel guides are available round the world.
For a copy of our current booklist or a list of our distributors write to:
Lonely Planet, PO Box 617, Hawthorn, Vic. 3122. Australia
Lonely Planet, Embarcadero West, 112 Linden St, Oakland,
CA 94607, USA